# PATTI'S PEARLS

ALSO BY **PATTI LaBELLE** AND **LAURA RANDOLPH LANCASTER**

*LaBelle Cuisine*

*Don't Block the Blessings*

# PATTI'S PEARLS

*Lessons in Living
Genuinely, Joyfully, Generously*

# PATTI LaBELLE

*and Laura Randolph Lancaster*

**WARNER BOOKS**

An AOL Time Warner Company

Grateful acknowledgment is given to quote from "Phenomenal Woman" by Maya Angelou, copright © 1978 by Maya Angelou, from *And Still I Rise* by Maya Angelou. Used by permission of Random House, Inc.

Warner Books, Inc., 1271 Avenue of the Americas, New York, NY 10020
Visit our Web site at www.twbookmark.com.
For information on Time Warner Trade Publishing's online publishing program, visit www.ipublish.com.

 An AOL Time Warner Company

Book design by Fearn Cutler
Printed in the United States of America

First Printing: October 2001
10 9 8 7 6 5 4 3 2 1

Library of Congress Cataloging-in-Publication Data
LaBelle, Patti.
    Patti's pearls : lessons in living genuinely, joyfully, generously / Patti LaBelle and Lauura Randolph Lancaster.
        p. cm.
    ISBN 0-446-52794-7
    1. Conduct of life. 2. LaBelle, Patti. I. Lancaster, Laura Randolph. II. Title.

BJ1581.2.L22 2001
170'.44—dc21

                                                            2001026873

*This book is dedicated to Zuri, my heartbeat, who has taught me so much of what I know about love—its patience, its power, its glory. In these pages may you find treasures worth more than gold, the secrets of living genuinely, joyfully, generously. And may they help you learn long before your mother did the ultimate secret of happiness: to grow wise before you grow old.*

# Acknowledgments

First and foremost, thanks to God for His boundless grace and blessings. And for allowing me to wake up each morning and say the words of Isaiah 12:2 without fear, hesitation, or doubt. *I will trust, and not be afraid: for the Lord Jehovah is my strength and my song; he also is become my salvation.*

Thanks to Jamie Raab, dream editor, who understood and believed in this book long before it was written—and who did all the right things with it once it was.

Thanks to Allen Arrow, whose knowledge of the law is equaled only by his knowledge of people—how to steer them, support them, and surround them with what they need when they need it most.

Thanks to Al Lowman for his belief in this book—and his tremendous skill at getting others to believe in it, too.

Thanks to Armstead Edwards for shepherding this

book through its many stages. But most of all for helping me show our son that respect shouldn't cease just because romance does—and that the end of a marriage doesn't have to mean the end of a friendship.

Thanks to Kristin Clark Taylor who helped in so many ways that only she knows.

Thanks to Reign, my rottweiler, who stays up with me whenever I can't sleep—and watches over me when I can.

And last but by no means least, a special and heartfelt thanks to my friend and collaborator, Laura Randolph Lancaster, who has a rare and special gift: the ability to turn words into music.

# PATTI'S PEARLS

*For wisdom is better than rubies;*
*and all the things that may be desired*
*are not to be compared to it.*

Proverbs 8:11

# Introduction

All my life people have told them to me. Pearls of wisdom worth more than rubies. "Sentence sayings" filled with the wisdom of the ages. Timeless truths that, if followed, hold the secrets of living genuinely, joyfully, generously.

It started when I was a kid. Every summer, when I visited my grandmother Ellen at her farm in Florida, she would tell them to me. From the day I arrived until the day I left, she would tell me some pearl of wisdom that usually went in one ear and out the other. "Bloom where you're planted, child," she used to say whenever I talked about all the things I was going to do when I got back home, back to the city, where we had all kinds of things—stores, televisions, *indoor plumbing*—that she didn't have in the country. "Do what you can, with what you have, where you are."

My mother did the same thing. To the tenth power.

Until she died, Chubby *never* stopped telling me pearls of wisdom. Words to live by. "God brings men into deep waters, not to drown them, but to cleanse them," she would always say when I was facing some crisis that I didn't know how to handle—or if I even could.

Almost thirty years later, my family and friends are *still* telling me pearls of wisdom. And they're some of the wisest things I've ever heard. Just a few months ago, for example, in the last conversation we ever had, my aunt Naomi told me some words of wisdom I badly needed to hear. They're in the book. But all I want to say about them now is this: I will treasure them my whole life as much for their wisdom as for what I know it took for Aunt Naomi to summon the strength to share them with me when she was lying in a hospital bed.

And while I've always *heard* these pearls of wisdom, only recently have I started to heed them. Live by them. *Abide by* them. That's because only recently have I come to understand their full meaning—and magic. I know what you're thinking: Why now? Why have these pearls of wisdom, pearls I've been told my whole life, suddenly become the blueprints for living it?

I've asked myself that question a thousand times, and I think there are two answers, really. The first is age, pure and simple. By the time you reach fifty-six, if you've paid attention at all, the School of Life has taught you a thing or three about how to live it. As the Bible says, "With the ancient is wisdom; and in length of days understanding." The second reason is a book. A book that made me look at myself and my life in a way I never had: my life story. Writing *Don't Block the Blessings* forced me to take a long, hard look at my life—the good, the bad, and the ugly. But more important, it forced me to try to make some sense of it. To look at my mistakes and what they cost me. To acknowledge them, accept them—and then come to terms with them. Some of those mistakes are in *this* book. The ones that I like remembering the least— but have taught me the most.

But let me explain why I'm bringing up *Don't Block the Blessings*. When I was writing it, that's when it started to happen. That's when I started to understand how much pain and heartache I could have spared myself—and a whole lot of other people in my life—had I done one simple thing: listen to the pearls of wisdom I'd been told from the time I was a little girl. Everything I needed to live the way we all want to—in peace, with passion and pleasure and purpose—all the secrets of living genuinely, joyfully, generously, I *knew*. Because at some point in my life somebody far wiser than I had told them to me. All I had to do was follow them.

If you've ever been to one of my concerts, there's a good chance you've heard me sing the song "When You've Been Blessed." I perform that song a lot because I love what it says: *When you've been blessed, pass it on.* This book is my attempt to do just that—pass on to others all the wisdom that others have tried to pass on to me.

Which brings me to something about this book I need to tell you. Something important. While it's called *Patti's Pearls,* I didn't write them. As I said, people far wiser than I did that. But, like so many of the pearls of wisdom we all grew up hearing—"A penny saved is a penny earned"; "Half a loaf is better than none"; "Don't count your chickens before they hatch"—I have no clue what wise soul actually composed them. And I doubt if the people who told them to *me* know either.

So why do I call this book *Patti's* Pearls? Because of all the timeless truths I've been told in my fifty-six years on this earth, the ones on these pages have made the greatest difference in my life. They have either spared me a whole lot of pain and heartache, or could have had I had the good sense to listen to them when they were first told to me.

I hope you will find as much wisdom in these pearls as I have. Because they can make all the difference in your life. As the Bible says, "Happy is the man that findeth wisdom, and the man that getteth understanding."

Be happy!

*The only time*
*you run out of chances*
*is when you stop taking them.*

In the seventies, right after Labelle broke up, I thought my career was in serious trouble. No, that's not true. It was much worse than that. In the months following the breakup of Labelle, I thought my career was over. Finished. Circling the drain.

You have to understand, I had been with Nona and Sarah for more than a decade—since we were teenagers—and just the *thought* of setting foot on a stage without them wrecked me. I mean, the mere idea left me paralyzed with fear. There was only one thing in the world more frightening to me than the thought of singing solo. And that was the thought of never singing again.

That's the only reason I finally agreed to perform a solo concert. Even then, my best friend, Norma, had to push me out on that stage. Literally. I had worked myself into such a frenzy, I probably wouldn't have lasted five minutes in front of that audience if I hadn't wrapped myself in the words Norma whispered in my ear as she shoved me into the spotlight: "You never run out of chances, Pat, until you stop taking them."

Thanks to Norma's words, words that reminded me that God wouldn't bring me that far only to leave me, I was able to reach deep down inside myself and give a performance that earned me a hand-clapping, foot-stomping standing ovation. Though it's been nearly three decades, every now and then I'll run into some-body who was at that show and they'll tell me, "Girl, you turned the place out that night." Unfortunately, I didn't learn the lessons of that experience until much later, after I'd turned down dozens of wonderful chances be-cause I was afraid to take one. After I'd said "no" to a whole lot of people and opportunities I should have said "yes" to. After I finally learned to see fear for what it re-ally is: False Evidence Appearing Real. Faith turned in-side out.

To make sure I never again let my fear of failure or

the unknown get the best of me, I repeat Martin Luther King Jr.'s brilliant words on the regular:

Fear knocked at the door.

Faith answered.

There was no one there.

It was Norma who tried to tell me what Brother Martin knew instinctively. He knew in his heart, in the marrow of his bones, what it took me half a lifetime to learn: If you wait until your hands stop shaking, you will never open the door. You can't steal second base by keeping your foot on first. You have to go out on a limb. Because that's where all the fruit is.

*Many a false step is made*
*by standing still.*

For the last several years, I was smiling on the outside and dying on the inside. That's how long I pretended my marriage was fine when I knew it was finished. That's how long I lingered in a relationship I knew I should have left.

Why I didn't leave sooner I'm only now beginning to fully understand. Part of it was because I didn't want to hurt my family; I didn't want to change their world just because I wanted to change mine. Especially since I was the one who had encouraged them to believe in a fantasy: that Armstead and I were the perfect couple. A modern-day Ozzie and Harriet. A real-life Ward and June. In reality, of course, nothing could have been further from the truth. In reality, Armstead and I were more like the Odd Couple than the perfect couple. More Oscar and Felix than Cliff and Claire.

While I didn't want to upset my loved ones, that's only part of the reason I didn't leave my marriage sooner. The main reason was less selfless, more spineless. The main reason I didn't leave sooner was to spare myself from making an agonizing choice, a choice I wanted desperately to pretend didn't exist: between hurting my son or healing myself. Between causing him pain or ending mine. Between starting to live for myself or continuing to live a lie.

That's how I justified staying. That's how I rationalized the happy marriage charade. That's how I handled everything—the loneliness, the emptiness, the pretense. Staying meant I wouldn't have to choose between breaking Zuri's heart and mending mine. At least that's what I told myself.

But the longer I stayed, the unhappier I became. And the unhappier I became, the more I started to understand what my friend Laura Nyro, the legendary singer-songwriter, tried to tell me many years ago when I was at another crucial crossroads in my life.

"Many a false step is made by standing still," Laura said to me when I told her that I wasn't going to leave Labelle.

Like a lot of people close to us, Laura knew that the

creative differences between Nona, Sarah, and me were destroying us. Deep down, I knew it, too. But instead of acknowledging the problem, I ran from it. Instead of facing the music, I stayed and suffered in silence. Until the day we broke up, I kept all the pain inside and pretended.

"You don't get it, do you, Pat?" Laura said to me one day when I called her in tears after a particularly ugly fight with Sarah and Nona. "Doing nothing doesn't get you off the hook. Because if you choose not to decide, you still have made a choice. If you choose not to leave, you have decided to stay."

I wish Laura were alive so I could tell her that, almost thirty years after that phone call, I finally get it. I finally understand what she was trying to tell me: Not to decide *is* to decide. Doing nothing *is* doing something. Silence is the door to consent.

You know the old saying "You can run, but you can't hide"? Well, it's a cliché for a reason. Take it from someone who's tried to run from her problems more times than enough. Enough to know it never works. And here's why. Because you can't hide from yourself. It's simply not possible. As the book title says, "Wherever you go, there you are."

As I've learned the hard way, if you choose to do nothing about your problems, you have actually made a deliberate choice. Because not saying "no" is saying "yes." Not saying "I won't accept that"—whether it's a bad marriage or an awful job or an abusive relationship—is actually saying "I will accept it." *Not deciding to progress is deciding to stand still.*

In my life, that single awareness has been worth its weight in gold. Because it has led me to an even greater understanding: Even if you fall on your face, you're still moving forward.

# *If you can't be the tablecloth, don't be the dishrag.*

I learned this principle from my mother, and the older I get, the more I appreciate its wisdom. Chubby—that's what everybody called her—insisted that everyone in her life treat her with respect. Though she wasn't wealthy or well educated, my mother not only understood and appreciated her value, but *believed* in it. Strongly. Deeply. Passionately.

As a result, Chubby never allowed anyone to treat her as though she were second best. And when I say anyone, I mean *anyone*. Not even the people she loved most in the world. Or I should say *especially* the people she loved most in the world.

Though she loved my father deeply, when she learned he was cheating on her, she insisted that he move out of our home. Not the next day or the next week. The very day Chubby discovered my father had gone back on his promise to be faithful to her, she told him he had to go. She couldn't forgive him, she said. Not again.

For months after she put Daddy out, he would come by the house on weekends to see my sisters and me. When it was time for him to go, we would beg Chubby to let him come back home. Her answer was always the same: not as long as I'm black and the sky's blue.

To me, as a child, Chubby's refusal to take my father back seemed harsh, even cruel. As a woman, however, I have come to understand it. For my mother, putting Daddy out of the house and her life wasn't about pride; it was about principle. The one she had always lived by. The one she believed in with all her heart. No one was going to love and respect you unless you loved and respected yourself.

Not long after Chubby and Daddy broke up, my older sister, Vivian, got involved with a married man named Charles. She and Chubby fought about it constantly. Although Charles's wife knew all about Vivian, Chubby couldn't deal with it. A few times, she and Vivian almost came to blows about it. Finally, Chubby gave Vivian an ultimatum: End the relationship or move out of the house. Vivian chose to move; a few weeks after that argument, she found an apartment and left.

Though Charles was truly devoted to my sister, in the seventeen years they were together, Vivian was never the only woman in his life. As much as Charles loved her— and he loved her deeply—the fact is Vivian always had to share him. Though the relationship had the acceptance, if not the blessing, of the only three people whose feelings really mattered—Vivian, Charles, and Charles's wife—that's something I don't know that you can ever really make peace with.

Over the years, I have told this story to more than a few friends who were either involved with or thinking of becoming involved with a married man.

"Even if you can get past the ethical problems," I warn them, "you can't escape the personal ones: When you date a married man, you will always, *always,* be getting another woman's leftovers. Her husband's leftover time, her husband's leftover attention, her husband's leftover money. No matter what lies he tells you, you tell yourself, or you both tell each other, you will never be his priority. His wife will always be the tablecloth and you will always be the dishrag."

Given the choice—and you always have one—I'd be the tablecloth, thank you. *Not* the dishrag.

*You don't need
a certain number of friends,
only a number of friends
you can be certain of.*

A lady of the night taught me this lesson. Her name was Corrine, and I met her at a club in London when Sarah, Nona, and I were living in Europe in the early seventies. Everything about Corrine was big—her mouth (she could curse like a sailor), her size (she was almost six feet tall), her heart (she'd give you her last nickel, which is pretty amazing when you consider the line of work she was in).

Corrine and I hit it off instantly. Girlfriend loved soul music and soul food almost as much as I did. Cooking up a big pan of macaroni and cheese on the stove while listening to Motown on the stereo was Corrine's idea of heaven. My best times in Europe were spent with her in the kitchen of a rented London flat cooking our favorite dishes, singing our favorite songs, sharing our deepest secrets.

I don't know if it's *because* of what Corrine did for a living or in *spite* of it, but I do know this: She had a sixth sense about people. Within five minutes of meeting you, she could read you like a book. If you were anything other than what you claimed to be, Corrine would know it. She could peep your game in a New York second.

Her assessments were never wrong, a fact she loved to remind me of. "Pat," she used to say, "I can spot a '2F' coming around the corner." A 2F was a "fake friend." That's what Corrine called people who tried to befriend celebrities for all the wrong reasons, everything from free tickets to a free ride.

When Labelle hit it big when we got back to the States (not *if* we did; Corrine said she knew in her heart it would happen), Corrine thought Sarah and Nona would be pretty good at spotting the 2Fs. But, if they had even a moderately good game, she thought they could fool *me* without too much trouble. "Pat," she used to say, "when it comes to people, here's what you gotta learn: Every relative isn't family, and every buddy isn't a friend."

Unfortunately, I had to learn it the hard way. And I won't lie: It was a painful lesson. One of the most hurtful of my life. I think part of the reason it hurt so much was that I honestly believed that all the "friends" I had when Labelle was riding high were just that: friends. Real ones. The kind who will stick with you through thin and thinner when there isn't any thick. The kind who, as Oprah says, will ride the bus with you when the limo breaks down.

As I would discover when Labelle broke up, nothing could have been further from the truth. These people gave 2Fs a bad name. As soon as the money and the hit records and the sold-out concerts disappeared, so did they. People who once gave me parties and presents and private phone numbers wouldn't give me the time of day. If I saw them out in public, they acted as if it hurt them to speak to me, as if I had something that Ajax wouldn't scrub off and penicillin wouldn't cure.

As with many painful experiences, this one turned out to be a blessing in disguise. It taught me a lesson I badly needed to learn. It taught me what the old folks mean when they say, "In prosperity our friends know us; in adversity we know our friends." And it showed me who my *real* friends were—the people who not only would ride the bus with me if the limo broke down, but would walk home with me if I was too broke to afford the fare. There weren't—and aren't—a lot of folks in that category; to this day I can count them on the fingers of one hand. But that one hand is enough. As Corrine always said, "You don't need a certain number of friends, just a number of friends you can be certain of."

# Your self-worth is more important than your net worth.

The money was major. Serious. Beyond belief. I'm talking the never-have-to-work-again kind that everyone dreams about. The kind that will take care of all of your debts and most of your dreams. The kind that can finance your future *and* your fantasies.

In the eighties, that's the kind of money I was being offered to perform in South Africa. A lot of artists were. Of course, when those offers were being made, the oppression of black people in South Africa was the law of the land. Shockingly, appallingly, a minority of whites controlled the lives of millions of blacks: Where they could live. What jobs they could hold. What kind of education they could receive.

Given that reality, for me, the answer was a no-brainer: No way, no how, no need to call me back. To my amazement, however, several promoters did just that. Not once or twice, but several times. And with every new call, they would sweeten the offer. Low six figures for several shows became high six figures for a few. High six figures for a few shows became seven figures for one. *One!* Before the calls stopped, the offer on the table was one I'd never heard before and haven't heard since: Name your price.

What the big-money boys didn't get was this: I didn't have a "price." As I have learned over the years, while money is important, it's not all about the Benjamins, as the hip-hop generation likes to say. There are some things you just can't put a price on. Things like your dignity, your values, your self-worth and respect. They should never—not ever—be for sale, I don't care how stupid the money is. Not if you want to be able to sleep at night. Not if you want to be able to look in the mirror and like the person you see.

You'd be surprised at the kinds of things I've been offered money to do. Everything from endorsing products I don't believe in ("Oh, don't worry, Miss LaBelle. No one will know you don't really use it") to lip-singing my live shows ("Only you and the band will know").

One of the sleaziest things I've ever been asked to do

happened early in my career when some powerful music executives offered me a sweet-as-sugar deal to sign with their label. Unfortunately, while the deal was sweet, the timing was rotten: I still had another couple of years on my current contract.

Apparently, I was the only person who saw that as a problem. As several music industry insiders informed me, if I wanted out of my contract, all I had to do was start acting like a pompous, spoiled, self-important diva. Miss deadlines. Make unreasonable demands. Treat people as if they were gum on the bottom of my shoe. A few months of tantrums, troublemaking, and terrorizing the folks I worked with and they would release me from my contract with pleasure. The strategy even had a name: BAB. For the uninitiated, that's "be a bitch."

Now I'm no Mother Teresa, but this was a seriously shady plan that I wanted no part of. When I said as much, several well-placed executives assured me my concerns were uncalled for. It was the kind of maneuvering that went on all the time, they said. Everybody did it. Everybody knew about it. Everybody looked the other way. Maybe they did. But, as I told those executives, that didn't make it right, just common. As I have learned over the years, a lot of people tune out the voice of conscience when money begins to talk. I just didn't want to be one of them. Not then. Not now. Not ever.

Of course, had I listened to other people instead of my conscience, it would have been easy for me to rationalize doing something that I knew I shouldn't: These people had years of experience, and I was just a rookie with no idea how things worked in the big leagues. If the top people in the business said BAB was standard operating procedure, who was I to rock the boat? And even if I did it this once, it was business, not personal.

Of course, that would have been the ultimate lie. There is nothing more personal than your values. What you will and won't do to get ahead, the lines you will and won't cross to win, whom you will and won't step on for personal gain, are at the very core of your code of honor. And your code of honor determines your character. And your character is who you are. Behind closed doors. When nobody is watching.

I'm happy to say that even way back then I understood doing what's right is always better than doing what's easy. Though it cost me a pretty penny, I told the music execs thanks, but no thanks. And I have never regretted it.

Compromising morals for money is *always* the wrong

choice. Because what you gain is never worth what you get. Why do you think when somebody stabs you in the back your fingerprints are very often on the knife? The answer is because once upon a time, in all likelihood, you did something similar to somebody else.

Peace of mind just can't be bought. Trust me: Even if your conscience doesn't stop you from playing dirty to get what you want, once you get it, it *will* keep you from enjoying it. As my mother used to say, "A good conscience is God's eye." Which is why I always prefer a loss to an underhanded gain; the one brings pain at the moment, the other for all time.

*Every exit*
*is an entrance to someplace else.*

Breakups, good-byes, any kind of ending—no matter how necessary I knew them to be, for most of my life they shook me to my core. That stopped a few years ago when I gained a precious understanding: Nothing ever ends without something else beginning. All beginnings *come* from endings. Every exit is an entrance to someplace else.

Until recently, I focused only on the endings. How much they hurt. How hard they were to handle. How much they upset the carefully constructed order of my life. When, for example, Zuri moved to California, I thought I'd never be happy again. I was so devastated that for weeks I walked around in a daze. I couldn't sleep. I didn't eat. And I cried all the time.

I knew exactly what was wrong with me. Of all the roles I was trying to fulfill—wife, mother, performer, friend—my favorite was mother. *Full-time* mother. That's who I thought the best part of me was. Mothering Zuri was what I did best.

So when my son, my *heartbeat*, moved across the country, it wrecked me. I was so focused on what I was losing (my kid, our routine, my identity), I couldn't see what I was gaining. And I was gaining a lot. The freedom to focus on my needs and wants. And, for the first time in more than twenty years, the time and space to fulfill them.

With Zuri on his own, a brand-new day in my life had dawned. But I couldn't see it, at least at first, because I was so focused on the door that was closing, I couldn't see the one that was opening. While the first half of my adult life was about learning who my son was and how best to take care of him, the next half was going to be about learning who I was and how best to take care of me.

A wise woman once told me, "We don't see things as they are; we see things as *we* are." Which is why whenever anything meaningful comes to an end—a marriage, a job, a cherished relationship—it's crucial to get the right perspective. As my aunt Hattie Mae says: "What the caterpillar calls the end, we call a butterfly." There's an old story I just love that really brings that whole point home. Two stonecutters were asked what they were doing. The first man said, "I'm cutting stone into blocks." The second man answered—are you ready for this?—"I'm on a team that's building a cathedral." Now boyfriend understood the power of perspective.

People ask me all the time, "Patti, why aren't you freaking out about your divorce? After all, you're breaking up with the man you've been married to for more than half your life." If my divorce happened ten years ago, I probably would be freaking out. But that's not my reaction now because I have learned to see the beginning in the ending. I have learned that a bend in the road is not the end of the road, as long as you make the turn.

Yes, my divorce means the end of my life as a married woman. But it also means the start of my life as a single one. A footloose-and-fancy-free, kids-all-grown-and-gone, it's-time-to-take-care-of-me single woman!

I'm not saying my divorce is easy; it's not. No end—at least to anything meaningful—ever is. But I'm not having a nervous breakdown over it because I have learned how to look at it. Not as an ending, but as a new beginning. Just as waking is an ending to sleeping.

# Rotten wood cannot be carved.

Sometimes faith can be a bad thing. I am referring specifically to the I-can-reform-anybody-if-I-just-treat-them-kindly theory to which, until recently, I subscribed unconditionally. As a result, I spent a lot of time and energy trying to change people into something they were not—and had no desire to be. Despite what my grandmother Ellen always told me, for most of my life I believed that you *could* make a silk purse out of a sow's ear. Or at the very least, a linen one.

There was ample evidence to the contrary, of course. But because I didn't want to see it, I either rationalized it away (she wasn't *trying* to be nasty; she just had a bad day) or ignored it. When, for example, a former employee who'd been fired for stealing wrote me to say (1) he wanted to make amends for any pain he'd caused;

and (2) since he'd been let go he'd been in and out of jobs and in and out of homes, I asked: "Have you learned your lesson; do you want your old job back?"

"Yes," he said—to both questions. Those of you who know about real life know where this story is headed. Less than a year later he was caught with his hand in the cookie jar—again. Well, not exactly *in* it, but trying to get the top off.

"It's not what it looks like," he swore. "I'm a Christian now; you have to believe me."

Believe it or not, I did. I know what you're thinking: Fool me once, shame on you; fool me twice, shame on me. I *know* that changing the label doesn't alter the contents of the bottle. But I believed deep in my heart that *everyone* was susceptible to improvement. That everyone was—or at least *wanted* to be—a decent human being. And if I worked hard enough to help a person become one, he would never let me, or himself, down.

That's why I was so floored—and hurt—when, several months later, my management team uncovered definitive-beyond-a-doubt proof of boyfriend's latest scam. (Trust me, you don't want to know the details.)

That's not the first time I got conned badly. There have been other scams, other stings, other swindles.

Frankly, a lot of people had to do a lot of things, rotten ones, before I understood what my grandmother Ellen meant when she said, "A rattlesnake will emit only poison, even though you feed it only honey."

Those experiences haven't made me cynical, but they *have* made me careful. I haven't stopped looking for the good in people. I've just accepted the fact that I'm not always going to find it.

"Rotten wood cannot be carved." I once laughed at that expression. But that was before I lived long enough to see its truth.

*Making a living
is not the same thing
as making a life.*

$\mathcal{T}$ruly amazing. That's the only way I can describe my career. All thirty-plus years of it. My work not only pays my bills, but feeds my soul. Singing fulfills me in ways I can't find words to express. Suffice it to say, I love it so much that I'd do it for free. (Note to my record company: Don't even think about it.)

That said, I never confuse my life with my life's *work*. As I have learned by personal experience, and many examples, a career—even one as wonderful as mine—is not what makes a satisfying life. Not by itself, anyway. One of the most important lessons I have *ever* learned, in fact, is that you can have all the professional success in the world and it won't be enough to make you happy.

Not completely. The big car, the big house, the big promotion, none of it will mean very much unless you also have a life outside of work. Unless you also have people you love and people who love you.

Early in my career, I missed a lot of special times with my family, times I'll never get back, because I didn't understand then what I do now. When Zuri was small, Labelle was trying to break into the big leagues and I was out on the road a lot. Birthdays and holidays were tough for everybody, but especially so for Zuri and me. Part of it was because we were separated during times when most families are traditionally together. And part of it was because I had to explain things that—to a child— are unexplainable: why Mommy wasn't going to be there to help him dye his Easter eggs or blow out his birthday candles or learn to ride his new bike.

One November afternoon, as I was packing to leave for a tour, my closest friend, Claudette, called me with what seemed like a strange request. "Patsy," she said, "you *have* to come home for Thanksgiving this year."

I gave Claudette the same answer I had given my family a few days earlier. "You know I wish I could, but this tour is a really important one for us. Maybe next year."

Claudette didn't say anything for a while. And when she did speak, her voice was very gentle, and very sad. "Patsy, friends and family should always come first. They don't read your résumé at your funeral."

I wish I could tell you that at that moment a light bulb went off in my head. That in that instant I "got" what Claudette was trying to tell me. The same thing a friend of some bigwig United States senator told him when the senator was diagnosed with cancer and decided not to run for reelection. I can't remember the senator's name, but I can't forget what his friend told him: "No man ever said on his deathbed, 'I wish I had spent more time at the office.'" That is so deep. And so true. Why do you think you've never seen a photo album filled with pictures of folks at their job—in meetings or conventions or conferences—*anything* to do with work?

What the senator's friend told him is exactly what Claudette was trying to tell me that long-ago day in November. But I didn't listen. And I paid a terrible price for it. That was the last holiday I ever had the chance to celebrate with Claudette. The breast cancer we all thought she had beaten returned. A few years later we lost her at the age of thirty-eight.

Only a very small, lucky number of people understand the wisdom of Claudette's words when they are young, as she was. Only a few of us have the smarts to understand what she was telling me sooner in our lives rather than later. I am not one of those people. Like most of us, it took me a long time to grasp what Claudette was telling me. And by the time I did, well, let's just say I'd spent more time building my résumé than I had building my relationships.

It works that way a lot, I'm afraid. Only when something terrible happens, something that reminds us how precious life is, how short and fragile, only then are we able to see what really is—and isn't—important. Only then do we get the gift Claudette tried to give me that Thanksgiving. The gift of perspective.

When a loved one dies or your kid gets sick, let me tell you how your perspective changes. All the things you thought were so important—that new contract and that corner office and that big promotion—don't mean diddly squat. When you're scared or hurt or lonely, only one thing matters. People. Those you love and those who love you. The people you can count on to hold your hand, to see you through.

I should know. There have been times in my life when I was so focused on my career that I had more Grammy nominations than I had friendships. Real ones, anyway. But, as I soon discovered, a Grammy Award is cold comfort when you're home alone and you hear noises in the basement. And it won't take you to brunch on your birthday or bring you chicken soup when you're sick, I don't care how hard you worked to win it.

I'm not saying that the benefits of professional success aren't real and rewarding. They are. But they won't make you happy, they won't *sustain* you, as you will find out the first time you sit down to eat Christmas dinner alone or you need to go to the emergency room in the middle of the night.

So the next time you're tempted to miss something important so you can stay late at the office—your anniversary or your kid's soccer game or a big family dinner—do me a favor. Don't. And when you're on your way home think about this: The most important things in life are not things.

Claudette would like that. And so would I.

# Save money, and money will save you.

You know the old adage about the best things in life being free? Well, it's true as far as it goes. The problem is, it doesn't go far enough. While no amount of money can buy you health, love, or inner peace, nobody talks about the flip side: Almost everything else you will ever need or want in this world costs money. A roof over your head. Food on your table. Health care for your family. Higher education for your children. Like it or not, you can't provide any of these basics for yourself, let alone your loved ones, without money.

I think most people don't talk publicly about the importance of money in our lives because they are afraid it will make them sound shallow or selfish or superficial. But whether we talk about it or not, the straight-no-chaser truth is this: Money matters. A lot. So while I'm not suggesting it could ever buy you happiness (if you doubt this for a second, think Princess Diana), trust me when I tell you that, in the real world, money is a crucial part of the mix.

How can I be so certain? Because I have been there many times when money made the difference between security and vulnerability, comfort and chaos, a life lived in peace and a life lived in peril.

I have been on the other end of the phone when the electrician said he was sorry my family had been without heat for two days but, freezing temperatures or not, he wouldn't even come *look* at the furnace unless I could hand him payment when he knocked on the door.

I have been so hungry, I cooked hot dogs on a light bulb because they were all I had to eat.

I have been in the hospital room when doctors said they were discharging my mother, but if I wanted her to live comfortably at home, she would have to have round-the-clock nurses.

I have been in too many places where people told me they had to choose between paying for their groceries or paying their rent, living like a pauper in retirement or working till they die, going to the doctor or going broke.

That's why, whatever your income, it's crucial that

you embrace the "save money" mandate. Learn to invest your savings wisely—so they work as hard for you as you do for them. Set financial goals and refuse to let anybody or anything keep you from reaching them. You have to plan ahead, sugar; it wasn't raining when Noah built the Ark.

Take care of your money, and, I promise, it will take care of you.

# Accept everything you are and nothing you are not.

People are always amazed when I tell them that the owner of my first record label took one look at me and said I'd never get a record deal. Not from him, or anybody else, for that matter. But that's exactly what happened. The head of Newtown Records, a rich white man named Harold B. Robinson, almost cursed out my friend Mo Bailey for having the gall to bring Sarah, Nona, Cindy Birdsong, who was a Bluebelle before she was a Supreme, and me to his studio for an audition. The problem, however, was mostly me.

Had Mo lost his mind? Robinson asked him moments after Mo introduced me as the group's lead singer. Didn't Mo know I didn't have a snowball's chance in hell of making it in the music business? Why was Mo wasting his precious time?

Robinson's assessment had nothing to do with my voice; in fact, he had never heard me sing. As he told Mo, the reason I'd never make it in the music business was my looks. "She's too dark and too plain," Robinson said. "And everybody knows a plain dark girl can't sell records."

Fortunately, Mo didn't have the heart to tell Sarah, Nona, Cindy, and me that our audition was over before it had even begun. So when Robinson walked out before we'd sung a single note, Mo acted as if his exit were no big deal. "Sing it just the way we rehearsed it, girls," our producer told us as Robinson disappeared up a flight of stairs.

And that's just what Sarah, Nona, Cindy, and I did. Less than halfway through the song, Robinson came running down the staircase as if the studio were on fire. In a way, I guess it was. Sarah, Nona, Cindy, and I were burning up the mikes. And Robinson knew it. Forget what he'd said earlier, he told Mo. My voice wasn't just good; it was golden. Robinson loved it so much, in fact, that he tried to get Sarah, Nona, Cindy, and me to sign with his label on the spot.

But what if Robinson hadn't changed his mind? What if, instead of telling Mo his "too dark and too plain" theory, Robinson had told it to me? *What if I'd listened to him?*

I shudder to think what might have happened had I accepted the negative labels Robinson tried to pin on me. It would have been years, if ever, before I tried again to sing professionally. I might never have made a record, never felt the exquisite rush I feel when I sing for an audience, never discovered my divine potential.

Accepting the labels other people try to tag us with is one of the most destructive things we can do to ourselves. Because once we accept those labels, we allow them to define us—what we can do, what we should want, what we can and can't have. We start considering what others think is right for us instead of using our own instincts and self-knowledge to make our own best choices.

Over the years I have learned that we can't live genuinely until we learn to disregard the labels and judgments of others. As some wise person once said, "You aren't what people call you, you are what you answer to." The better we become at ignoring whatever people call us, the closer we get to fulfilling our dreams, the easier it becomes to create the life we really want, not the life someone else thinks we should have.

Three things are certain: Life's too short to live for other people. (I wish someone had told me *that* in my twenties.) And this, too: Life doesn't come with a rewind button. If we want to live genuinely, we have to free ourselves from the beliefs, attitudes, and judgments of others. We have to strive to be our truest self. We have to hear and heed the advice of Children's Defense Fund founder Marian Wright Edelman: "You were born God's original. Try not to become someone's copy."

# *Know God, know peace;*
# *no God, no peace.*

$\mathcal{I}$'m a Jesus girl. Always have been, always will be.

From the time I was a little girl singing in the choir of the Beulah Baptist Church, God has been my anchor, my life raft. My whole family and half my neighbors worshiped at Beulah. My sisters and I were baptized inside its sanctuary, and it was there, singing for the congregation on Sunday mornings, that I first felt the power and the glory of God's love. And I have never forgotten that feeling.

Throughout my life, whether my problems were unpleasant (big trouble with the bill collectors) or unbearable (big trouble with my marriage), somewhere deep in my heart I've always known God's love would get me through. That when there's no one else I can call on, I can call on Him—for grounding, for guidance, for grace.

Though I grew up in the church, I don't go much anymore. Years ago, some high-ranking church officials made me feel unwelcome because, they said, I was singing the devil's music. Their comments hurt, and hurt badly. But, as with most painful experiences, it taught me something important: I don't need to be *in* church for God to be in me. And I don't need to *go* to church in order to strive to live my life as He would want me to. As a wise person once said, "Going to church doesn't make a person a Christian any more than going to a garage makes a person a car."

Don't misunderstand; I have nothing against the church—nothing against its ceremonies or the many wonderful people who attend and perform them. I do, however, believe that everyone should develop a personal relationship with God. A direct line to The Creator. A one-on-one connection that doesn't depend on anything but faith to exist.

"From your mouth to God's ear." In my experience, that's the best way to get your prayers heard. And, more important, answered. When it's just you and God, you can talk to Him wherever you are, whenever you need to. No third parties, no special chants or channels, are needed. All you have to do is quiet your mind and still your soul so that you can hear The Holy Spirit clearly, without distraction, interruption, or interference.

It's a sweet thing, faith. With it, you can handle any circumstance, any crisis, because you know God always has your back. And when God is for you, who can be against you? Nobody. As my aunt Hattie Mae says, "One and God are a majority."

Without faith, however, life is a whole different movie. Without faith, it's easy to let your fears get the best of you. Even easier to listen to your doubts. Without faith, for example, I might never have found the nerve to start a solo career after more than ten years with Sarah and Nona. I know I wouldn't have had the courage to start a solo life after more than thirty years with Armstead.

I love what the Bible says about faith—that it is the substance of things hoped for, the evidence of things not seen. When my older sister, Vivian, was dying of cancer, I saw how that evidence could make the difference between peace and panic. I saw how faith could wipe out fear. As Vivian used to say, "When you believe in God, Patsy, death is a doorway, not a wall. And while I may have cancer, it doesn't have me."

When I'm facing challenges, when I'm going through

changes, I think about my sister's words. I remember that when you take your troubles to God, you may have them, but they don't have you.

Make God your management consultant. As one of the sisters at Beulah Baptist Church used to tell me, "Make sure the part He plays in your life isn't the spare tire, but the steering wheel." That's one of the best secrets I know for living genuinely, generously, joyously. That, and pray every day—you cannot stumble when you're on your knees.

# *Barbie is a doll,*
## *not a goal.*

*F*or years, I longed to be thin. Notice I did not say I wanted to be thin or I wished I were thin or I thought it would be nice to be thin. I said I *longed* to be thin—as in hungered after (and believe me, hungered is the right word here).

Notice also that I did not say a healthy weight or a fit weight or the right weight for a woman my age and size. I said *thin.* Runway thin. Barbie doll thin. *Thin thighs* thin. I also wanted Tyra Banks's boobs, Naomi Campbell's legs, and Halle Berry's hips. In short, I wanted The Look.

The Look, as every woman knows, has three essential elements: perky breasts, tiny waist, and a butt you can bounce a quarter off of. If you need a visual, just picture one of the models in the Victoria's Secret catalog. It doesn't matter which one; they *all* have The Look, which my friend Diane refers to as "the Triple B"—"body by Barbie."

As Diane was fond of telling me, getting The Look wasn't a healthy or realistic goal for me—or any woman over the age of nineteen—to have. Deep down, I knew she was right. For years, friends in the fashion business had told me that, if translated into human proportions, Barbie's measurements would be *38-18-34!* But that didn't stop me from wanting it anyway.

Since I hadn't seen nineteen in quite some time, in my efforts to get The Look, I did some pretty crazy things. I went on off-the-wall diets (believe me, sugar, you don't want to know). I spent a small fortune on lingerie (if it promised to tie it up, tuck it in, or tape it down, I had to have it). I even downed a fair amount of—how can I put this?—"mysterious" tonics and brews. (I don't think any of them contained rattlesnake tongue or eye of newt, but I couldn't swear to it.)

And why did I torture myself this way? Because I believed the hype. I bought into the American beauty myth, that mass-marketed idea that beauty comes in only one shape (hourglass) and one size (six). The truth, of course, is that is the ultimate lie. Whatever else you may be sure of, be sure of this: When it comes to beauty, *one size fits all.*

This realization has given me a whole new attitude about beauty—my own and other people's. I call it "the phenomenal woman" attitude, and a twentysomething saleswoman in a lingerie shop inspired it. Neither thin nor beautiful in the classic sense, girlfriend seemed to glow from within. She radiated self-assurance and joy. For more than an hour, she said nothing as she helped me struggle into undergarments with names like "the Stomach Smasher" and "the Butt-Be-Gone" (no, I did not make those names up, and yes, I bought them both).

It wasn't until I was home putting away my purchases late that night that I saw it. The note this wise-beyond-her-years saleswoman had taped to one of the boxes. "Miss LaBelle," it read, "it was a thrill to meet you. You are such a beautiful person—on the inside and out. I hope you enjoy your purchases—and that you won't be offended by my sharing with you something my mom always told me: Barbie is a doll, not a goal."

Wow.

Talk about profound. Girlfriend knew in her twenties what I didn't figure out until my forties. She knew that what makes a woman beautiful isn't about size (although

I'm not going to lie: You can't let your weight get so out of control that you need Omar the Tentmaker to make your clothes); it's about sight. Not how *other* people see you, but how *you* see yourself. That a woman's value is that which she sets upon herself. That if you put a small value on yourself, the world will not raise your price. Which is why you must think highly of yourself, because the world takes you at your own estimate.

Most important, she knew that what makes a woman beautiful isn't necessarily even physical. Maya Angelou, the *original* phenomenal woman, explains this truth so brilliantly in her poem of the same name:

> *Pretty women wonder where my secret lies.*
> *I'm not cute or built to suit a fashion model's size*
> *But when I start to tell them,*
> *They think I'm telling lies . . .*
> *I say,*
> *It's in the arch of my back,*
> *The sun of my smile,*
> *The ride of my breasts,*
> *The grace of my style.*
> *I'm a woman*
> *Phenomenally.*

*Phenomenal woman,*
*That's me.*

And the moment you gain that precious understanding, I promise it will be you, too.

*The best way
to predict your future
is to create it.*

In the early eighties, my future as a solo artist was in serious doubt. After Labelle broke up, I recorded five albums in as many years, and I don't think any one of them cracked the Top 1,000, forget the Top 10. For whatever reason, I couldn't buy a place on the charts.

When my third album sank without a trace, if I ever came close to giving up my career, it was then. I pictured myself twenty years later, still wearing those silver spacesuits Labelle made famous, traveling from city to city playing the oldies but goodies circuit. In my suitcase, I'd have three or four tapes of me singing my new music, which I'd take out and play when life got too depressing. I'd tell myself that it wasn't too late for me to make it on my own, that solo success was just around the corner, that it was just a matter of time before I hit it big. Looking back, I think that vision of my life and myself drove me a little crazy. I *know* it's why I started begging God to send me a miracle—a hit record, a brilliant producer, something, *anything,* to turn my career around.

Armstead made a huge difference during this awful period. Since I couldn't *give* my albums away, he suggested that I accept an invitation to star in the gospel musical *Your Arm's Too Short to Box with God.* Well, that was the last thing I wanted to do. Not because of the play, because of me. When I perform live, I let the spirit move me. If I feel like kicking off my shoes or rolling on the floor, that's what I do. When I'm onstage, nothing is scripted; I let the mood and the moment drive me.

As you can imagine, that doesn't go over real well in the theater, where the success of the performance depends on everybody following a carefully plotted script. But I was so desperate, I let Armstead talk me into doing it. And I'm so glad he did. After nine months touring the country, *Arm's Too Short* made history when it opened on Broadway for the *third* time. No other musical had opened on the Great White Way so many times in such a short period.

While starring in a hit Broadway show is great, the lessons that whole period taught me are far greater. And what it taught me is this: First, if you always do what you've always done, you'll always get what you've always got. You know the old saying "If at first you don't succeed, try, try again"? Well, it *should* say, "If at first you don't succeed, figure out what you did wrong, *then* try, try again."

And the second thing I learned is that having faith doesn't mean asking God to give you what you want, then sitting back and waiting for Him to send it. God doesn't do the work *for* you; He does the work *through* you. It's not enough to look *up;* you must also look *within.*

As my girlfriend Llona used to say, "Patsy, don't grow a wishbone where your backbone ought to be. Say 'I will,' not 'I wish.'" Listen to Llona, that's what I say. It's fine to pray for a good harvest, as long as you keep plowing. And always remember: You are the *s/hero* of your own story. We all are. Which is why you have to pray as if everything depends on God, but work as if everything depends on you.

*In matters of the heart,
it is always better to want
something you don't have than to
have something you don't want.*

This is a big one. It's so big, in fact, that I'm going to say it as bluntly as I can: If you want an unhappy life—and this is a guarantee—get involved with a man merely for the sake of having one. As any woman who has ever done just that can tell you, the relationship is doomed from the start. However badly you may want it to work, however much you may want it to last, it won't. Not even if you twist yourself into a pretzel trying to force it to.

I don't know how long it will take for it to happen, but it will: One day you will wake up and realize that all the effort and energy it takes to sustain this kind of relationship is sapping your spirit, dragging you down. That being involved with the wrong person is a thousand times harder—more annoying, more frustrating, more trying—than being by yourself.

In some ways, I owe my first glimpse of this truth to Temptations founding member Otis Williams, whom I almost married when I was in my twenties. Back in the sixties, Otis was what was known in my grandmother's day as "a catch." Smart, kind, rich, and famous, boyfriend was all that and a bag of chips. When we were a couple, I can honestly say I loved Otis. Which was why when he asked me to marry him, I said "yes." I wasn't *in* love with him, however, which is why I didn't.

It could be wishful thinking, but I really do believe that, deep down, Otis knew we weren't right for each other, too. If he didn't know it, he sure did a great job of acting as if he did. The day I broke our engagement, Otis accepted my decision with true grace, a kindness for which I will always be grateful.

I thought of that day not long ago when a friend called and told me she'd resigned herself to the fact that she was probably never going to find Mr. Right, so she was going to marry Mr. Right Now. It seemed to me that day on the phone, and on all the days I stayed in a marriage I should have left long before I did, that nothing kills the dream or the possibility of a good relationship quicker than the realities of a bad one. Or a settled-for, second-rate, time-to-let-it-go one.

There are few things that I can say with certainty about love and relationships: When the person you spend your days and nights with isn't the person you really want, when the things he brings to the relationship aren't the things you really want or need, you will soon see the "someone is better than no one" theory for what it is: a crock. You will soon understand what it took me many years to learn: In matters of the heart, it is always better to want something you don't have than to have something you don't want.

It's not just that the relationship won't fulfill you. It's that it will make you unhappy, desperately so. Because every day, in some way, it will disappoint and disillusion you. And when you've been disappointed and disillusioned enough times, that is when you will get it. What I tried to tell my girlfriend that day on the phone: Getting married when you're *in* love is called settling down. But getting married when you're not is just settling. And, as someone who did the second instead of the first once told me, when you've settled, a wedding ring is the smallest handcuff in the world.

# Don't try to change the wind, change the sails.

It will come as no surprise to anyone who has ever seen me cook or eat that I do not like being a diabetic. No, that's not true. I *hate* being one. But that doesn't change the fact that I am. Like it or not, it's the hand life has dealt me. Once upon a time, that fact would have made me crazy. Every day, in some small way, I would have worried about it, complained about it, seethed about it, stressed out about it. And you know what? It wouldn't have changed a thing. At the end of the day, I'd *still* be a diabetic. Just an upset, frazzled, stressed-out one.

I've had enough rotten things happen to me to know that, when something bad happens, something you can't do anything about, it's hard to wrap your mind around the fact that it's futile even to try. But you *have* to; it's the only way you will ever know any peace.

I won't lie: There are still times when I forget the wisdom of this truth. If the blow is bad enough, it can be almost impossible not to. When, for instance, I first learned I was diabetic, I freaked out. I cried about it for days, and I went into denial about it for weeks. I might still be in denial if it weren't for my friend Cassie and what she did when we were having lunch together a few months after my doctor called me and gave me the news. Before we ate, Cassie asked if she could bless the food; only instead of giving a traditional grace, she softly recited the Serenity Prayer.

*GOD*
*grant me the*
*SERENITY*
*to accept the things*
*I cannot change*
*COURAGE*
*to change the*
*things I can*
*and the*
*WISDOM*
*to know the difference.*

Every woman should have that prayer on her wall. If you looked at that prayer every day and asked yourself, Is this problem something I can do anything about? you'd waste a lot less time railing against all the stuff life deals you that you cannot change.

But let me get back to Cassie. After she recited the Serenity Prayer, she told me something I didn't want to hear but needed to: She told me I couldn't change my condition any more than she could change hers. That just because she didn't want to have a painful, chronic condition with no known cure didn't mean she didn't. As Cassie explained, she had recently been diagnosed with a disorder of the intestines called "irritable bowel syndrome." In addition to being extremely painful, it was also often disabling, because, among other things, the condition causes constant bloating and frequent diarrhea.

"We can't *change* our condition, Pat, but we can learn how to live with it," Cassie said. "I can control the symptoms with medication and diet, and you can do the same. If you want to be at peace, don't try to change the wind, change the sails."

Whether it's diabetes or a sick friend or a broken heart, everybody gets his share of heartache. It's called "real life." And I can't promise you the pain won't be bad; at times it may be so bad, you will feel it pulling you down. But when it does, I want you to remember what Toni Morrison says: "If you surrender to the wind, you can ride it."

# Look at life through the windshield, not the rearview mirror.

My sister Barbara tried to teach me this lesson more than twenty years ago. At the time, she was planning her wedding under what I can only describe as bittersweet circumstances. On the one hand, my sister was about to realize a life-long dream: At age thirty-eight, she was about to marry the man she had been in love with since they were teenagers. On the other, she had just been diagnosed with colon cancer.

I am convinced that when my sister was planning her wedding, she knew the clock was ticking. Not that she acted like it. On the contrary, Barbara acted as if she didn't have a care in the world. Given the seriousness of her illness, you can understand why her cheeriness freaked me out. However cheery Barbara *acted*, the hard, cold truth is that she didn't have a cold, she had *cancer*.

Given that reality, I assumed my sister would call off her wedding. I mean, how could she stand up and say the words "till death do us part" when she knew how close her death could be? But calling off the wedding was the last thing on Barbara's mind. As I watched in amazement, she went about the business of planning the ceremony as if all was right with the world.

Part of me thought Barbara was nuts, and part of me thought she was in denial. As it turns out, my sister was neither. As I would come to learn, the only one who couldn't see the truth was me.

For weeks, I kept my feelings to myself. I had to. At Barbara's request, I was hosting the wedding reception and I knew she wanted me to be as excited about her big day as she was. One afternoon, however, I just couldn't keep silent any longer. To this day, I'm not sure what made me snap. Barbara and I were going over the reception details—the food, the flowers, the friends she wanted to invite—when I had a meltdown. I lost it.

I started sobbing like a baby. "It's so unfair. You and Shot finally get your chance and what happens? You get cancer. What about all the years you've lost? What about all the time you may never get? Doesn't just the thought of it make you crazy?"

Barbara wiped the tears from my face. "What good would it do to be angry, Patsy?" she said gently. "I can't change the past and I can't control the future. I can, however, make the most of the present. Shot and I are together *now*. At this moment. And, if you think about it, this moment is all any of us really has."

The ability to live fully in the moment—in the time and place we are right now—is one of the greatest secrets I know of living joyfully. Because once you grasp it, freedom is very close. You stop worrying about the past and stressing out about the future. Enjoying life—not agonizing about what happened yesterday or worrying about what might happen tomorrow—becomes your priority. Your days become a gift, not a grind.

In September 1980, Barbara and Shot exchanged wedding vows before God, family, and their closest friends. Two years later my sister died. But what an amazing two years they were! The happiest, I think, of Barbara's life. Of this much I am certain: Before my sister passed, she squeezed every ounce of joy out of every single moment. She didn't spend her time dwelling on the past or worrying about the future. She looked at life through the windshield, not the rearview mirror. She *lived*.

More than anyone I have ever known, Barbara understood the power of living in the moment. That life is in session *now*. That we can't choose how we're going to die. Or when. But we can choose how we're going to *live*. Thanks to my sister, I understand that fear of the future is a waste of the present. That if you look back too much, you'll soon be heading that way. Because if we fill our hours with regrets of yesterday and with worries of tomorrow, we have no today in which to be happy. And that today is a precious gift, that's why they call it the present.

*Money is a universal provider
for almost everything but happiness
and a universal passport
to most any place but heaven.*

*A*s I've said earlier, if you want your money to take care of you, you have to take care of it. While I'm hardly a financial expert, at its most basic level, I think taking care of your money comes down to two simple rules: (1) Spend what you have left after saving, instead of saving what you have left after spending; and (2) Don't leave your financial future up to fate or chance. Where money is concerned, nobody plans to fail; they just fail to plan.

That said, there's a third fact about money that we all need to understand. A fact you need to be clear about if you are to live generously and joyously. *It is a means to an end,* not an end unto itself. Money has no innate, built-in worth. In, of, and by itself, money isn't worth diddly.

I have known too many people in my life who didn't understand this truth. People who looked at money as an end instead of as a means. As a result, they never enjoyed the things their money could bring. All they ever did was work to accumulate more of it and then hoard it when they did. Eventually the wealth they possessed came to possess them.

So, after "Save money, and money will save you," here's my most important dictum on dollars: Money is worth only one thing—what you can trade it for. And you should never—not ever—be afraid to trade it for things that make you happy, things that can make your life fuller, richer, sweeter.

Money speaks a language everyone understands. It's a universal provider for most everything but happiness and a universal passport to most any place but heaven. Spend it accordingly. Because you sure can't take it with you. You've never seen a Brink's truck following a hearse. And I'm willing to bet you never will.

*Women who want to lead the orchestra have to turn their back on the crowd.*

on't do it; you'll regret it as long as you live."

With few exceptions, primarily my family, that's the advice everyone gave me when I was struggling to make the most important decision of my life: whether to go through with my pregnancy or end it.

Now, I'd made difficult decisions before, but they were nothing like this one. This one made me question who I really was and what I really wanted. This one pushed me as far as I could possibly go.

When I learned I was pregnant with Zuri, Patti La-

Belle and the Bluebelles had just pulled off a miracle. Against all odds, we had transformed ourselves from a group on the verge of extinction to a group on the verge of superstardom.

It wasn't easy. Hardly. After more than a decade on the chitlin' circuit, Sarah, Nona, and I were as broke as church mice and going nowhere fast. Desperate, we moved to Europe, where we spent months "reinventing" ourselves. We changed everything—our look, our lyrics, our image, our sound. To my shock and amazement, our transformation from R&B old-school group to rock 'n' soul new age group worked. Our music and our message hit young America's nerve. In the early 1970s, Labelle became the new "It" group. Just as we'd always dreamed.

And during those heady days, a dream is just what my life felt like. Labelle was the darling of the music industry; my husband, Armstead, and I were moving to a music that was all our own; and Sarah, Nona, and I had never been closer. Then I got pregnant. And things were never the same.

The day I announced the news, I got one of my first tastes of the seedy side of fame: the ugly power it can have over people. The unthinkable things it can make them do. If I heard it once, I heard it a thousand times: "Get an abortion, Pat. Now, before it's too late. What's important is Labelle's career, not whether you do or don't want this baby."

No one put it that bluntly, of course. But what they *did* say—that having my baby would be professional suicide, that rock stars were lovers, not mothers, that a pregnant lead singer would destroy Labelle's hipper-than-hip image and everything we'd worked for in the process— sent the message loud and clear.

I'd like to tell you that I never gave ending my pregnancy a first, or even second, thought. That I told everybody who urged me not to have my baby to talk to the hand. I'd like to tell you that, but I would be lying. The truth is this: This was not a planned pregnancy. Armstead and I planned to have children someday, but both of us agreed that day wouldn't be any time soon. So not only did I think about ending my pregnancy, but I thought about it seriously.

The stress I felt, the guilt trips I took—my God—I just felt like a beat-down, smashed-up rag doll. But through it all my inner voice stayed strong. It didn't waver. It didn't care. *Have your baby,* I heard with complete clarity and felt with complete conviction.

I was lucky. I listened to myself. I trusted my heart. The day Zuri was born, I was so thankful I hadn't listened to everyone else that when the doctor put my baby in my arms, I almost turned that hospital out. You know how loud I sing? Well, that's how loud I cried. Hysterically. Frantically. Uncontrollably.

I tried to hold it all in, but I couldn't. When I saw my son's face, it was as if a dam inside me burst. Everybody thought I was overcome with happiness. And I was. But more than anything, I was overcome with gratitude. As I held my baby boy, all I could think was, Thank You, Lord. Thank You for this child who is here today because You let me hear my truth.

I haven't always heard it as clearly. Well, that's not exactly true. I've always heard my truth, but there have been far too many times in my life when I didn't listen to it. Far too many times I was so worried about taking care of other people's needs and desires that I ignored my own.

Now that I'm on the other side of fifty, though, I don't do that anymore. Now that I'm on the other side of fifty, you know what I finally figured out? That we never need to look outside ourselves for the ultimate answers. That our own instincts about what is best for us are always better than somebody else's. Because our own instincts are always more in touch with our deepest needs. Always. Do you hear?

It's like what country superstar Reba McEntire says. You can always feel what is right for you better than others can. The best decisions you ever make in your life happen when you go with your gut feelings. Reba should know. Like me, she says she stayed in an unhappy marriage—her first one—long after her inner voice told her she should leave.

"I heard the voice and had the gut feeling, but it took a while for me to make the move," Reba says. "As soon as I did, I knew it was right."

It always is. Which is why, if you can learn to hear and heed your inner voice . . . well, nothing else much matters. That's what women who lead the orchestra know. That's what women who turn their back on the crowd understand. That's what women who lead their best lives do.

*You preach a better sermon
with your life
than you do with your lips.*

This truth doesn't require a lot of explanation. The only thing I'd add to it is this: "Well done" is always better than "well said." Because people may doubt what you say, but they'll always believe what you do. And they take your example far more seriously than your advice. So let your life speak for itself. And when it does, don't interrupt.

# Treat your body like a temple, not an amusement park.

There are two things in this world I love almost as much as singing: cooking and eating. Since I was a kid, both have been great passions. Both are in my genes. You see, I come from a long line of great Southern cooks. I'm talking about folks whose food was so fabulous, meals so magical, dishes so divine, that just smelling them could make you start speaking in tongues. "The torch of love is lit in the kitchen," my aunt Naomi used to tell me when I was a little girl. Toward that end, I've spent as much time in front of a stove as I have in front of a stage.

So when I tell you I understand the siren call of food—its pull, its pleasure, its power—I'm not just blowing smoke up your stove. A food fan to the depths of my soul (and stomach!), I know from where I speak.

As a kid, instead of selling Girl Scout cookies, I ate

them. Until recently, I went out on three A.M. cheese-steak runs as often as I went out on tour. (Hey, I'm from Philly, the home of the ultimate cheesesteak.) Whether I was eating it or cooking it, my food philosophy was as simple as ABC: $Appetizing = Butter + Cream$ sauce.

Counting calories or fat grams didn't interest or faze me. In the kitchen, the only thing I counted was help-ings—how many I was going to eat and how many I was going to serve. Butter, cream, and sugar weren't ingredi-ents to be used with moderation; they were ingredients to be used with abandon. The holy trinity of LaBelle cuisine.

Then one day a few years ago I got a wake-up call. Literally. After a routine physical exam, my doctor phoned me one morning and dropped a bomb. I had di-abetes. The disease that had killed my mother. The sick-ness that had stolen her spirit. The illness that had taken her legs and, soon after, her life.

Gently but firmly, he gave me a choice. I could con-trol my diabetes by changing my diet—cut the calories, retire my fryer, say "sayonara" to the sugar and the sweets. Or I could continue my old eating habits and let my diabetes control—or kill—me. The choice was mine, he said. But before I made it, he wanted me to know this:

If I continued my old eating habits, dying before my time wasn't just a possibility; it was a likelihood.

His bottom line? If I wanted to regain control of my health, I had to eat right, exercise, and maintain a healthy weight. To make sure I understood how serious he was about the healthy weight part, my doctor ran down a long list of illnesses linked directly to obesity—high blood pressure, heart disease, and stroke, to name a few. "Patti," he said when he finally came up for air, "you've got to eat to live, not live to eat."

And that's just what I'm doing. My three A.M. cheese-steak runs are a thing of the past. I can't remember the last time I had a Blimpie and a beer. My six-cheese macaroni and cheese is no longer a staple at my Sunday dinner table. In fact, unless I'm cooking for company, many of my most requested dishes—Lasagna LaBelle, Burnin' Babyback Ribs, Say-My-Name Smothered Chicken and Gravy—only make rare appearances on my table. (I'm not going to lie: I had to wean myself off my fried chicken and potato salad *slowly.*)

And just so I don't have to rely on self-control when a sugar craving hits me at midnight (*real* foodies know that's when ice cream and cake taste best!), I don't even buy sweets anymore. While I'll walk down to the kitchen to get some pound cake, walking to the bakery, or *anywhere* outside my house, for that matter, is out of the question, I don't care how bad my sweet jones is.

If diabetes has taught me anything, it's that obesity isn't just a cosmetic problem; it's a health hazard. And not just for diabetics. I'll spare you the medical mumbo jumbo, but let me put it like this: More people commit suicide with a knife and fork than with any other instrument. That's because, diabetic or not, being overweight substantially increases your chances of developing all kinds of treacherous, potentially lethal conditions. The kind that can take you away from here before your time.

Fortunately, the path to good health isn't paved with rice cakes and spring water. You don't have to starve yourself until you look like one of those skinny little nineteen-year-olds they put on magazine covers. (Is it just me, or do they look like giraffes with hair and breasts?) Study after study has shown that just a small drop in weight—I'm talking a measly ten pounds—can make a real difference in your health.

Since I learned I was diabetic I've dropped a dozen. Now, that may not *sound* like a lot, but you have to consider this: Not only do I feel better since I lost the weight, on a good day I can fit into one of my mermaid gowns.

I love those dresses! They hug your body so tight that if you have a pimple on your behind, everybody in the audience will know it. The other night I wore one to close a show and, while I don't want to brag, let me just say that Morticia didn't have a thing on me.

All kidding aside, while doctors don't agree on much, on this point there is no debate: Eating to live is the most important thing we can do for ourselves. Eating to live is our best chance for a long and healthy life.

*Coincidence
is the pseudonym God uses
when He doesn't want to sign
His name.*

How many times have you "accidentally" run into someone you'd just been thinking about? Or been thinking about someone at the exact moment she called? How many times has information you've been searching for come to you right when you needed it?

I've experienced all of these "coincidences" and more. A lot of people have. But, after a truly amazing experience, I had to stop chalking up the "coincidences" in my life to chance. Without getting all Deepak Chopra on you, I have come to believe that coincidence is one of the ways God reveals Himself. The pseudonym He uses when He doesn't want to sign His name.

The experience I'm referring to is so incredible, so far beyond chance, that it would be almost too fantastical to believe if it hadn't actually happened. But it did—at my baby sister's funeral. All week I'd been a basket case. By the middle of the service, I was having a lot of trouble holding myself together, and I wasn't sure I was going to make it to the end. I wasn't being a drama queen; I had every reason to be sick with guilt. I've told this story a thousand times, but in case you haven't heard it, I didn't grant my sister's last wish. I promised to do it later. But later never came. Jackie died before I got around to taking her the only meal she wanted when she was going through the chemotherapy treatments: an egg sandwich.

At her funeral, I was so crazy with guilt that almost everything about the service is a blur. Everything, that is, except this: a little yellow butterfly. Throughout the service, it fluttered around the church. You have to understand how eerie and amazing that was, what a truly strange "coincidence." As anybody who knew my sister could tell you, Jackie had always had a thing for butterflies. As a kid, she spent hours behind our house chasing them. She thought they were the most beautiful creatures she'd ever seen.

Which is why a butterfly flying around the church at her funeral would have been incredible enough. But it's what that butterfly did before the pallbearers carried my sister out of the church that made me know that "coincidence" is one of the many ways God moves and directs our lives, if only we are willing to let ourselves be guided. As the minister was finishing the eulogy, that butterfly came to me. It flew across the church and landed on my shoulder. For a few moments, it just sat there. And then it flew away.

Call it what you want—delusion, illusion, grief-induced confusion—but I know what I saw. And I don't believe anything about that experience was a coincidence. What I *do* believe is this: Out of all those people in the church, that butterfly came to *me,* it landed on *my* shoulder, because Jackie wanted me to understand something that I badly needed to know. That she had forgiven me. That I shouldn't torture myself about what happened. That all was well with her—and us.

Most of our reactions to the things that happen in our life are nothing more than habits. Thanks to that butterfly, I've stopped the habit of dismissing the "coin-

cidences" in my life as flukes of fate. Instead I pay attention to them. Bear witness to them. File them under
"Everyday Miracles." Because that's what I believe they
are. And, if we let them, they can reveal things to us that
we badly need to know.

# Resign as general manager of the universe.

This pearl of wisdom is truly special to me, as my aunt Naomi told it to me in the last conversation we ever had. She'd been feeling poorly for a couple of weeks and had gone into the hospital for observation and tests. I was about to go out on the road for several weeks, so I called to see if she wanted or needed anything before I left. "No, Patsy," Aunt Naomi said. "I'm going to be fine real soon, baby."

There was something about the way she said it—something about the certainty and serenity in her voice—that made me think Aunt Naomi knew something about her condition that the doctors didn't. That she knew no matter what they would or wouldn't find or what they could or couldn't tell her, it wouldn't be long before she'd be seeing Chubby, her best friend for more than thirty years, again.

We were both right. Shortly after that phone call, Aunt Naomi died.

While I know in my head that Aunt Naomi is no longer with us, where it counts—in my heart—it's hard for me to believe she's gone. Part of it is because her death is so recent; she died just six months ago. But most of it is because Aunt Naomi is the only family member I grew up with who lived into her seventies. And though we weren't related by blood, Aunt Naomi *was* family. From the time I can remember, she was like a second mother to me. Until I was a grown woman, she lived with my family, and from the time I was a little girl she treated me as if I were her own.

When I was little, she used to bathe me in the kitchen sink, and I was the only person on this earth, Chubby included, whom Aunt Naomi shared her secret recipes with. I'm talking about the fly-you-to-the-moon ones. The make-you-wanna-holler-and-throw-up-both-your-hands ones. The ones people would offer to do *anything* for.

But let me get back to our last conversation. A few days earlier, a friend of Aunt Naomi's said something to her that Aunt Naomi said she wished someone had told her when she was a young woman instead of an old one.

By her own admission, however, even if someone had given her this particular piece of advice when she was young, Aunt Naomi said one of two things probably would have happened: She wouldn't have understood it, or she wouldn't have listened to it. (I can *so* relate to that!)

When her friend gave her this advice, Aunt Naomi was doing what she'd done ever since I'd known her: trying to solve somebody else's troubles. That's how she was. If somebody in her life had a problem, Aunt Naomi would do everything in her power to fix it. And I mean *everything*.

As Aunt Naomi was listing all the things she was going to do to help this person, her friend stopped her in midsentence. "Naomi, girl," she said, "you need to re- sign as general manager of the universe. You need to learn that sometimes the best way to help a person is to let them help themselves. Otherwise, they never learn how. And they are always going to make *their* problems *your* problems."

After she told me about that conversation, Aunt Naomi was quiet for a long time. But the silence—and her next words—gave her thoughts away. "You need to learn that, too, Patsy," she said quietly.

We all do. And I'll be the first to admit I probably need to learn it more than most. In an effort to do just that, I often read the words George Peters, a dear friend since childhood, sent to Armstead and me when he heard we weren't just separating temporarily, we were divorcing. George knew in addition to all the strains of the divorce, a lot of other stuff in our life was going less than smoothly. What he didn't know, however, is that the day he sent the words I'm going to share with you, I'd had my "resign as general manager of the universe" conversation with Aunt Naomi.

Not the day before or the day after. The *same* day. As I said, there are no "coincidences."

Every time I read these words, they cool me right out. If you take them to heart—and taking them to heart is the key—I know they'll do the same for you.

*GOOD MORNING!*

*This is God,*

*I will be handling
all of your problems today.
I will not need your advice.*

*I will not need your suggestions.*
*The only thing I will need from you is*
*your cooperation.*
*So, relax and have a great day!*

*A thousand mistakes*
*are an education*
*if you learn something*
*from every one.*

A few years ago I was complaining to my aunt Hattie Mae about all the mistakes I have made in my life. Big ones, small ones, stupid ones, serious ones—as I told my aunt, in my fifty-plus years on this earth, I've found a way to make every kind.

What triggered my outburst was, of all things, a song. Not one of those "three hanky" numbers about heartache and heartbreak and love gone wrong. No, the song that triggered my outburst was about the opposite experience: finding a soulmate when you least expect to. Falling in love again when you thought you never could.

As anyone who has ever heard it knows, "Nobody's Supposed to Be Here" is one of those emotional ballads that can make grown folks cry. As sung by the lovely and talented Deborah Cox, it's nothing short of beautiful, which is why it went platinum shortly after it was released and spent weeks at the top of the charts.

But the beauty of the song isn't what got to me that day. Hearing it made me remember something I wanted to forget: my decision *not* to record it, despite the fact that it was written especially for me.

"I could have had a number one single with that song," I half sobbed, half screamed, to Aunt Hattie Mae before launching into a bunch of other not-so-great decisions I'd made that year. Her response shocked me. Instead of sympathizing with me, Aunt Hattie Mae read me the riot act. I mean she let me have it with both barrels. First of all, she said, a worm is the only thing that can't stumble. Surely I was old enough to know *that*. But more important, I shouldn't be sorry about my mistakes, I should be grateful for them. Trial and error is the way we learn. *Making* mistakes wasn't my problem; the way I viewed them was.

Like most people, Aunt Hattie Mae explained, I saw my mistakes as failures—setbacks and defeats to disappoint, depress, or demoralize me. What they really are, however, are opportunities. Because it is from our mistakes that we learn the lessons we need to develop and grow.

And then she got *really* deep. "Child, don't you know that our wisdom comes from our experience, and our experience comes from our mistakes? And if there's one thing about the school of experience you can be sure of, it's that it *will* repeat the lesson if you flunk the first time. So stop your whining. The most valued people in the world are people with experience. And the more of it the better. So all you need to remember is that experience is the name everyone gives to their mistakes."

As I said, Aunt Hattie Mae got deep. But I was in way too much of a funk to listen to what she was trying to tell me that day, no matter how much sense she was making. Over the next few weeks, however, I thought long and hard about what she said. And the more I thought about it, the more I knew my aunt was right. When we make a mistake, if we keep the *lesson* and throw away the *experience*, we are smarter and wiser for it. At a minimum, we know what doesn't work, even if we haven't figured out what will.

Mistakes aren't just our teachers; they're also our motivators. They cause us to reexamine our choices, revise our plans, and, in some cases, reconsider the way we live our life. And change it for the better. For example, letting people take advantage of me more times than I can count compelled me at long last to learn to stand up for myself. And missing my chance to grant my baby sister's dying wish put an end to my habits of procrastination and indecision.

Not cooking Jackie that egg sandwich is one of the worst mistakes of my life. But because I kept the lesson and threw away the experience, it made me a better person. A *much* better one. Before the egg sandwich, I was Procrastination Princess, Queen of Delay. Now I don't put off doing anything I consider important. Because now I know what Aunt Hattie's sister, my aunt Joshia Mae, meant when she said, "You can never do a kind deed too soon, because you will never know how soon it will be too late."

Yes, my mistakes have landed me on my behind more than a few times. More times, I'd bet, than most. But as Aunt Hattie Mae said, that's a good thing, maybe a great thing. Because you know what I finally figured out? She who makes no mistakes doesn't usually make anything. And when you learn to see your mistakes for what they are—compulsory education—the harder you fall, the higher you'll bounce.

# You can't be a doormat if you don't lie down.

As a reformed doormat and recovering approval addict, I think I've earned the right to say this straight out. Besides, it's such an *essential* recipe for living genuinely, joyfully, and generously, I don't want there to be the *slightest* chance of misunderstanding.

Before I say it, though, I want you to breathe deeply. In, out. Okay, here goes: There is only one reason people take advantage of you. One reason they ask you for the kinds of "favors" they wouldn't dare ask anyone else. One reason and one reason alone that they manipulate and exploit you. *Because you let them.* And you let them for the same reason I did. Because you crave approval. *Because you want everybody to love you.*

I wanted everybody to love *me* so badly that for years I let other people's plans and priorities run my life. I allowed others to take from me without giving back, to goad or guilt me into solving their problems, to use me for their own ends, all because I was scared of losing their love and approval. Watching other people use me used to drive my friend Llona crazy, although she was the first person to tell me that it was my own fault. "Patsy," she used to say, "make yourself a sheep and the wolf is ready."

And she was exactly right. What life has taught me is that letting people take from you without giving back is as futile as it is unhealthy. Repeat after me: Unconditional indulgence does *not* lead to unconditional love. If my considerable experience with the first has taught me anything about the second, it's that one has nothing to do with the other. Not one single thing.

People who *really* love you don't put conditions on their feelings. They don't say, "I'll love you as long as you do what I want you to." Or, "I'll love you on the condition you continue to please me." Or, "I'll love you if you say 'yes' to everything I ask you to do." They say, "I love you"—period, end of sentence.

Since I reached this understanding, it's impossible to overstate how different my life is. How much richer and fuller and *easier*. While I'm not insensitive to the needs and wants of others, I have learned how crucial it is to honor my own.

I no longer think I have to say "yes" to every request. Even better, I have learned to say "no" without guilt or apology. Not, "No, unless you really need me to." Or, "No, if you promise you won't get mad at me." Whereas I once felt I couldn't turn down *anybody* for *anything,* at least not without offering an explanation why—why I can't loan them the money, why I can't come to the party, why I can't get them fifty tickets to a sold-out show—I now live by a very different philosophy. The " 'no' is a complete sentence" philosophy. The "you can't be a doormat if you don't lie down" philosophy. The "sticky label" philosophy. I will elaborate.

A few years ago a friend told me something some big-time female psychologist said that changed her life. I can't remember the head doc's name, but I do remember what she said. And what she said is this: "Remove those 'I want you to like me' stickers from your forehead and, instead, place them where they truly will do the most good—on your mirror!"

It took me fifty years to do that, mentally and literally. So do me a favor. Put down this book and put up your sticker. Today. This moment. Right now.

# They're the Ten Commandments, not the Ten Suggestions.

*I*'m going to let this one stand by itself. Its message is as clear as it is wise.

*You can't smooth out the surf,
but you can learn to ride the waves.*

I know what it feels like when tragedy strikes. I lost all three of my sisters to cancer when they were in the prime of life. Not one of them lived to see her forty-fourth birthday. Not Vivian, not Barbara, not Jackie. Neither did my best friend, Claudette; cancer took my sister-in-spirit when she was only thirty-eight.

The pain of losing four of the people I loved most in the world almost drove me mad. Their deaths were so sudden, so tragic, so swift. I didn't have the slightest idea how to cope with such heartache. Not a scintilla of a clue. I wondered why they had to die, why they had to suffer so terribly before they did, why God took them when they were so young and beautiful and full of life.

For years I tortured myself with those questions. What I finally realized is that only God knew the answers. Almost twenty years later, I can't honestly say I'm over their deaths. Truth be told, I don't think I will ever be. At least not completely. But I have survived them. I have gotten through them with my soul in one piece, something I once thought I'd never be able to say. Time doesn't always heal, but it makes the hurt bearable.

I've suffered a lot of other losses. Painful ones. Everything from the death of my parents to the death of my marriage. And since I've survived the worst of them, since I've walked through hell and come out the back door, I'm going to tell you as much as I know about how to do it. I'm going to tell you the most important thing I have learned about getting through all the bad stuff life deals you with your soul, if not untouched, at least intact.

It comes down to this: Bad things, tragic things, can happen to anyone. And they *do* happen to almost everyone. You can't stop them, you can't avoid them, you can't explain them, you can't control them. And you can't ask for bad things *not* to happen. All you can do is ask God to give you the courage and the strength that you need to handle them when they do. And then trust in your heart that He will.

Here's the thing about faith: It gives us the strength

to go on when we want to give in. It gives us the courage to get up when we want to lie down. It gives us the power to make a way out of no way when there ain't no way. Just as love can't make you strong until love has made you weak, well, faith can't lift you up until life has knocked you down. With faith or without it, we can't stop the waves. But *with* it, we don't need to. Because with it we can ride the surf.

*Anger is like the blade
of a butcher knife—
very difficult to hold on to for long
without harming yourself.*

I used to hold on to my anger. Nurse it. Feed it. Tend it like a garden. It didn't matter who (friend, family member, stranger) or what (a fight, a slight, an insult, real or imagined) had ticked me off. Weeks, sometimes months, after the incident I'd still be seething about it. I'd analyze it, replay it, relive it—and each time I did, I'd feel hurt and outraged all over again.

And while I was going through all of these changes, what was the person who'd ticked me off doing? Going on with his life. Nine times out of ten, not only was I the only one stressing out about the incident, I was the only one *thinking* about it.

The person who had (choose as many as you like) hurt me/insulted me/ticked me off either didn't know he had done any such thing, or he knew it but didn't care. Either way, my anger was my problem, not his.

Here's a perfect example: Years ago, Madonna and I were involved in a hit-and-run—pedestrian style—at the American Music Awards. In her zeal to get across the room to talk to a well-known singer, the Material Girl nearly ran me over. Though she almost knocked me down, to my amazement, Miss Thing kept right on going. She didn't stop to apologize. She didn't stop to see if I was all right. She didn't *stop*.

I tried to brush it off, but in my mind I was yelling, *Do the words* home training *mean anything to you?* To tell you the truth, I don't know if I was more angry or hurt, but I stewed about it for months. A year later, when I spotted Madonna at an all-star AIDS benefit in Los Angeles, I *still* hadn't gotten over what happened. The moment I saw her, I knew I had to tell her how much the incident had bothered me.

Well, guess what? Girlfriend didn't even remember it. Yes, she listened politely and apologized profusely. And yes, I do think her apology was sincere. But I also think Madonna didn't recall running into me at the show. Not really. And for nearly a year I'd been all bent out of shape over something girlfriend couldn't even remember happening! Confucius says, "To be wronged is nothing unless you continue to remember it." I say truer words were never spoken.

That whole Madonna experience taught me four important lessons about anger. The first is that, when you hold on to it, the only person you're hurting is you. I didn't really understand that until my aunt Joshia Mae broke it down for me in the most basic terms: "Patsy," she said, "holding on to anger is like eating poison and then waiting for another person to keel over." Deep, huh?

The second is that when you refuse to allow your anger to consume you, when you let it go and move on, what you are really saying to the person you are angry with is, "You no longer have the power to control how I feel."

The third is that the person you are angry with isn't thinking about you. Yes, I know, you are sure that they are either gloating about what they did to you and laughing behind your back or are spending most of their days trying to figure out how best to apologize and make things up to you. But they're not. The person you are angry with isn't even *thinking* about you. She is thinking about *herself* and going on with *her* life—just as you should be.

And the fourth is that every moment you are angry you lose a minute of happiness. At my age, that's just something I'm not willing to do.

*The smallest deed*
*is greater*
*than the grandest intention.*

It's taken me nearly thirty years to embrace my half-sister, Monica. While we're close now, until recently we were more like strangers than sisters. Part of the reason we stayed so distant for so long is that we were grown women before we had the chance to get to know each other. When my parents went their separate ways, Daddy moved out of state and started a new family. At best, I saw them once or twice a year.

But the biggest reason it took me so long to embrace Monica has nothing to do with distance or Daddy. The biggest reason is that even when I had the opportunity to spend time with Monica, I didn't take it. Even when she asked me to make a place for her in my life—and in my heart—I didn't. Not until it was almost too late.

My decision to keep Monica at a distance had nothing to do with her. Rightly or wrongly, I honestly believed that I couldn't get close to *anyone* in Daddy's new family without hurting my mother. Badly. Seriously. Deeply. So whenever Monica reached out to me, whenever she called or wrote or asked if she could visit, I was polite, but I never let her into my world.

I'm not sure why Monica kept trying so hard to be a sister to me. Why, *for years,* she never stopped reaching out to me. But I'm glad she did. Even before I spent any time with her, I had a feeling about Monica. Something inside me told me she was special. Kind. Caring. Real.

After my mother died and I knew it wouldn't hurt her, I promised myself I was going to do the only thing Monica had ever asked of me: spend time with her. Get to know her. Let her into my life. And I told her as much every time she called me (regularly) or I called her (not so regularly).

Unfortunately, while I was good at talking the talk, I was rotten at walking the walk. I was always *promising* to make time for us to spend together "one of these days." But, as I learned from Monica, in reality, one of these days is none of these days. In my defense, let me say that it's not as though when I told Monica we were going to be spending a lot of time together I was *lying*. I *intended* for us to do just that. In fact, I had all kinds of grand plans for the two of us: a week of pampering at some fabulous spa, an extravagant April in Paris vacation, to name just two. But grand *plans* were all they ever were. Promises I was always making ("I'll call you later"; "We'll go next month"; "You can come visit soon") but never kept.

Until, that is, I got The Letter.

Though it was five pages long, it basically said two things:

I don't care about fabulous spas or trips to Paris. I don't care if we sit on the curb and eat beans and count buses. What I *do* care about is spending time with you. And unless and until you feel the same way, don't call me anymore with your grand schemes. Don't call me anymore *period*.

It was signed:

"I really mean it,

Monica"

I've omitted all the parts that made me cry: all the promises I'd broken, all the plans I'd canceled, all the pain I'd caused. But as soon as I got myself together, I made two calls. The first was to Armstead, so he could clear my calendar for a week. And the second was to Monica, so I could ask her to come spend it with me.

To my surprise and delight, she did. And for seven days and nights we partied! We didn't do anything extravagant or grand, unless you count the Mimosas every morning and the raspberry truffle cheesecake every night. (Don't roll your eyes; this was *before* I learned I was a diabetic.)

But, as Monica always said, we didn't *need* to do anything grand. Just as a word of encouragement during failure is worth more than a whole book of praises after success, small deeds done are always better than great deeds planned.

*Blowing out another person's candle won't make yours shine any brighter.*

When I was a little girl, I used to stand in front of my bedroom mirror and sing Dinah Washington's songs into my hairbrush. Don't ask me why, but before I was old enough to even understand what the blues were, her voice stirred something deep in my soul. Her music *moved* me.

I loved it so much, in fact, that when I first started performing live, I always closed my shows with one of her signature songs, "Where Are You?". I don't know who loved that song more, the audience or me. But I do know I never sang it without getting a standing ovation.

It never occurred to me that Dinah Washington would have a problem with my singing that song. I assumed she would see my decision to close my shows with it for what it was: a tribute *to* her, not an attempt to take anything *from* her. Not that I could have even if I'd wanted to. I mean, let's be real. At the time, I wasn't even a blip on the music industry's radar screen, while Dinah Washington was music royalty. The Queen of the Blues. Which is why when I learned she had sent me a message, I was beyond excited, I was *thrilled*.

For one thing, I couldn't believe the great Dinah Washington had even heard of me. For another, I thought/hoped/wished she would invite me to be her guest at one of her shows. I was so excited, I let my imagination run wild. I dreamed up this whole fantasy about what would happen when we met. After the show, Dinah and I would go to her dressing room, where she'd tell me how flattered she was that I was singing "Where Are You?". Then she'd take me into her confidence—singer to singer, sister to sister—and share a tip or two about the art of live performance. Before I left, the great Dinah Washington would be more than my idol; she'd be my *friend*.

Well, as I said, it was a fantasy. There was, however, one part that was real. The part about her wanting to give me a tip about performing. Dinah Washington told me to stop singing her song.

Throughout my career I've encountered more people than I care to remember or count who sent me similar messages. I've had curtains dropped on me in midbow (headlining acts thought the applause I was getting was a little too loud). I've been asked to tone my voice down until it was, if not inaudible, at least indistinct (otherwise I'd deflect too much attention from other performers). I've even had my microphone shut off while I was in midshow—in mid*song* (years later that one still hurts).

I thought about those incidents not long ago when a friend brought an aspiring young singer back to my dressing room after a show. She was close to signing her first record deal and asked if there were any words of wisdom I could share with her at the beginning of her career, anything about fame I thought she should know.

I told her what my mother told me when I was a teenager singing in the Beulah Baptist Church choir. After the service, everybody in church would make a big fuss over me. Especially the sisters. "Patsy," they would say, "you've got the voice of an angel. Your solos are so pretty they could make a sinner see Jesus."

My mother never said anything in front of the sisters. But once we got home, Chubby made sure I understood something far too many people don't: *Glory is never diminished by being shared.*

"You're not singing by yourself, child," Chubby

would say. "Next time you're standing there soaking up all that praise, I want to hear you give the choir some respect. If I've told you once, I've told you a thousand times. A whole bunch of candles can be lit from one without diminishing it. Now, I know it's nice to have people treat you like a queen. But, unless you know how to wear it, a crown only has to fall a few inches to be a noose. Don't you ever forget that."

I never have.

*Sometimes*
*you have to disappoint others*
*to be true to yourself.*

I know how much it hurt my family when Armstead and I agreed to go our separate ways. Especially our sons. When we finally broke the news, Zuri and my two adopted sons, Dodd and Stanley, handled it like the sophisticated, rational, poised young men they are. Though they expressed deep disappointment at our decision to divorce, they did so coolly, calmly, evenly. There was no screaming, no shouting, no "how could you do this to us" recriminations.

Afterward I was really relieved. But I was also really worried. I didn't want my sons to do what I had done for so long—swallow my pain, hide my hurt, bury my feelings in order to spare someone else's until they were so deep inside me that I could no longer recognize them. I wanted Zuri, Dodd, and Stanley to let their emotions out. To tell me everything they were feeling, even if it was the last thing a mother wants to hear: how much this divorce has shaken their faith in their parents, themselves, their world.

As much as I'd like it to be otherwise, I know it has done all three. I don't care how calm, cool, and collected they act, they're human and I know this decision has turned their world upside down. But I also know something they don't: how much it was hurting *me* to stay in a marriage that had been dead for at least a decade. Even though Armstead and I had known for a long time that what was broken between us couldn't be fixed, it had taken us years to be able to admit it—to ourselves, to our family, to each other.

"When it becomes more difficult to suffer than change, you will change." That's what my friend Diane used to say whenever things got really rough, whenever I felt I was right there, on the brink, on the edge of an emotional abyss widening—and waiting—to swallow me whole.

But that's not even the worst part. The worst part is I couldn't see any way out. For years I told myself that divorce was out of the question. Not because *I* couldn't handle it, but because it would hurt too many people I loved too deeply. Especially Zuri. On those rare occasions when Armstead and I danced around the subject of temporary separation, even *that* didn't seem remotely possible, not with Zuri and Stanley and Dodd and my mother-in-law and so many people's feelings hanging in the balance. Yes, *maybe,* one day, I told myself—when the boys were married and had families of their own. But not before; maybe not ever.

So what made me change my mind? Two things, really. It became more difficult to suffer than change. And, just as Diane promised, when it did, I changed. On a day no different from any other, I told Armstead I wanted a divorce. He said he understood, then admitted he wanted one, too.

Why that conversation happened when it did, I'm not really sure. My theory is that everybody has a different threshold of endurance. All I know for sure is that I finally reached mine. As I said, there was nothing special about the day I reached it—no big blowup, no nasty argument, no ugly drama. I'd just had all I could stand of the loneliness and the emptiness. All I could take of waking up every morning feeling like a penny waiting for change.

The second thing that happened is this: I realized

that no matter how hard I tried, I couldn't make everybody in my life happy all the time. Not if I wanted to stay sane. That sometimes you have to disappoint others to be true to yourself. *And that's okay.* For me, that has been a life-changing realization—a kind of thunderbolt, "praise the Lord, glory hallelujah, let peace be still" flood of release and relief.

The opposite, I have come to understand, is also true. Just as I'm not in charge of anyone else's happiness, no one was put here to be in charge of mine. That's my job. And I'm getting pretty good at it. Because I finally understand what my friend Laura Nyro meant when she told me these incredibly wise words: "She who trims herself to suit everyone will soon whittle herself away."

*The only people to get even with are those who have helped you.*

The Bible tells us that vengeance is The Creator's business, not ours. And even if that weren't the case, as some wise person once said, "You can't hold somebody down without staying down with them." So I let God handle His business. And when I'm tempted to do otherwise, I remind myself of this undeniable fact: When you're getting kicked in the butt, it means you're in front!

# Don't spit into the well— you may have to drink from it.

Anybody who has been in show business for more than a minute—artist or executive—can tell you that your fortunes can turn on a dime. One day you can be running the company's errands, and the next day you can be running the company. One day your career can be so high that you can't even *see* the ground, and the next day it can be so low that you have to look up to see bottom. In my nearly forty years in the business, I've been on the mountain high and in the valley low, so I know from where I speak. And while I can't speak for "the suits," I can tell you that there's usually a cycle to an artist's career. People go from saying, "Who's Patti LaBelle?" to, "Get me Patti LaBelle," to, "Get me a young Patti LaBelle," to, "Who's Patti LaBelle?" over and over again. You can't get too high or too low in any phase of the cycle, because as soon as you do, it's all going to change.

Young singers ask me all the time, "Miss LaBelle, what's the secret of staying hot in this business?" I tell them what I just told you. You can be the most talented person on the planet Earth, but you're never going to be hot *all the time*. There's always going to be a new "It" girl. Fair or not, that's just the way it works.

So why am I telling you this? Because life is like that, too. One day everything can be fine, and the next day everything can be funky. One week you can be on top of the world, and the next week the bottom can drop out. If we live long enough, we're all going to get our share of bad times. It's called "real life." And while the bad times *will* pass in the by-and-by, I have found that getting through them is so much easier if you have done this one simple thing: treated people with kindness, dignity, and respect. *All the time*. Not just when you need them. Not just when they can do something for you. Not just when they're up and you're down or when they're riding in the limo and you're riding on the bus. *All the time*.

People ask me all the time why I treat people so nicely. What they really mean, of course, is why I treat people they don't consider important—taxi drivers, waiters, grocery store clerks—so nicely. The answer is because we're all God's children. And for that reason alone, common courtesy and basic respect are the least we owe each other. As my aunt Joshia Mae says, "To belittle is to *be* little."

But I also tell them another fact of life. I've lived long enough to know that in life, as in show business, you never know who is going to end up where. The grocery store clerk you are rude to today could be your boss tomorrow. The woman you disrespect in the morning could be the nurse at the hospital where you have to leave your mama in the evening.

In short, the toes you step on today might very well be connected to the behind you may have to kiss tomorrow. Which is why you should never spit in the well; you just never know when you'll have to drink from it.

*The trouble with a woman standing behind her man is that she can't see where she's going.*

I went from my mother's house to my husband's house. From a young girl being taken care of by her family to a young woman being taken care of by her man. Until I was a grown woman in my fifties—fifty-six, to be exact—I'd never lived alone. Never driven a car. Never faced a day, or a disaster, on my own. Even so, until my marriage ended, I didn't really understand what America's "Sister President," Dr. Johnnetta B. Cole—the first African American woman to head Spelman College, the nationally esteemed historically black college for women—meant when she said, "The trouble with a woman standing behind her man is that she can't see where she's going."

Now that I'm on my own, however, I understand it completely. Until my marriage ended, I'd never taken full responsibility for much of anything in my life—not its direction, not its decisions, not its day-to-day details. With my blessing, for more than thirty years, my husband managed everything—our finances, our family, our house, my career.

As a result, in the months following our breakup, I was lost. I had stood behind Armstead so long, I could no longer see where I was going. And when it came to my business affairs, I sure didn't know what I was doing. What I knew about them you could have fit in a thimble, with space to spare. And so, during one of the most difficult and emotionally draining times in my life, I had to begin to learn everything it took to run my life. And when I say everything, I mean *everything:* The basic stuff (my monthly bills and how to pay them). The not-so-basic stuff (my career options and how to weigh them). The stuff you have to deal with now. Today. In the here and now—insurance policies, retirement plans, savings strategies—if you want your life to run smoothly later.

Control of my business and financial affairs wasn't

the only thing I surrendered during my marriage. I also gave up many of the things that brought me joy. Things I loved but I knew Armstead hated. Things I pretended weren't important to me if they weren't important to him. Things that made me happy and made him crazy.

Like dancing the night away, for example. If the music is good and the party is pumping, I want to stay until the deejay spins the last record. Armstead is just the opposite; he usually wants to leave by midnight. And during our marriage, leave the party is just what I did. Not always, but most of the time. No matter how much fun I was having, no matter how badly I wanted to stay, when Armstead said he was ready to go, I'd get my coat and get to stepping.

Now let me be clear: Armstead never forced me to leave a party, or anywhere else, before I was ready. He didn't force me to give up any of the things I loved. I chose to. I chose to go along to get along.

Far worse than the parties I gave up, however, were the people. Girlfriends I once hung out with on the regular, I didn't give the time of day. Friendships that were once important to me became irrelevant to me. All the things girlfriends do to stay close, to remain connected— lunching together, shopping together, gabbing on the phone together—I stopped. Where I once held them close, I held them at a distance. Eventually, women I once shared so much with, friendships that had once been an important source of joy in my life, disappeared. There wasn't any drama connected with the disappearances—no clashes, no confrontations, no come-to-Jesus conflicts. The friendships just died on the vine of neglect.

That's another lesson I've learned the hard way. *All* relationships will die if they aren't nurtured. Just as a flower will die if it's not watered. Because love is demonstration, not declaration. Or, as country singer Clint Black puts it, "Love is a verb, not a noun."

With every passing year, I lost more than friendships. With every passing year, I lost big chunks of myself. Whole pieces of my personality, the things that made me an individual, the quirky little stuff that made me an original, I gave up to keep the peace. I'm not sure when it happened, but one day I woke up and I didn't know who I was anymore. I couldn't distinguish between me, the real me, and the mask I wore.

Now I'm trying to reclaim all the missing parts of myself. I feel like I'm finding my voice. Unearthing my essence. The other day, when a friend told me what Jane

Fonda said when she separated from Ted Turner, I knew exactly how she felt.

"Being without a man is allowing me to remember what it feels like to live in my own skin," she said. Me too. And it feels good. Really good. Because for the first time in my adult life, I'm exploring my needs, my dreams, my desires, all of which, in one way or another, will lead me on the journey of my lifetime—a journey home to myself.

*Give yourself to God;*
*you can be sure*
*He will take care of what is His.*

Of all the pearls of wisdom in this book, this one is my favorite. Because it says clearly and simply all you really need to know to live genuinely, joyfully, generously. The only thing I would add is this: Whenever times get hard, when you don't know how you got wherever you are, let alone how you're going to make it out—out of the pain, out of the heartache, out of the terrible sorrow or situation you find yourself in—remember that God never built a staircase to nowhere. And when you do what you can, He will do what you can't.